THE PORTABLE CRAFTER
CARDMAKING

PEGGY JO ACKLEY

A LARK / CHAPELLE BOOK

A Division of Sterling Publishing Co., Inc.
New York

A Lark/Chapelle Book

Chapelle, Ltd., Inc.
P.O. Box 9255, Ogden, UT 84409
(801) 621-2777 • (801) 621-2788 Fax
e-mail: chapelle@chapelleltd.com
Web site: www.chapelleltd.com

10 9 8 7 6 5 4 3 2 1

First Edition

Published by Lark Books, A Division of
Sterling Publishing Co., Inc.
387 Park Avenue South, New York, N.Y. 10016

Distributed in Canada by Sterling Publishing,
c/o Canadian Manda Group, 165 Dufferin Street
Toronto, Ontario, Canada M6K 3H6

Distributed in the United Kingdom by GMC Distribution
Services, Castle Place, 166 High Street, Lewes, East Sussex,
England BN7 1XU

Distributed in Australia by Capricorn Link (Australia) Pty Ltd.,
P.O. Box 704, Windsor, NSW 2756 Australia

Manufactured in China

ISBN 13: 978-1-57990-981-9
ISBN 10: 1-57990-981-7

For information about custom editions, special sales, premium
and corporate purchases, please contact Sterling Special Sales
Department at 800-805-5489 or specialsales@sterlingpub.com.

TABLE OF CONTENTS

INTRODUCTION

Receiving a handmade card or tag says something about both the maker and the recipient. In this fast-paced, mass-produced world, the realization that someone took the time to make a card with their own hands for a special person or a special occasion is something to be savored and saved. Greeting cards communicate feelings, and a hand-made card can express something beyond words.

In this book there are various handmade card and tag projects to make for celebrations, holidays, and "just because." You will find that creating these small jewels of art-work is an extremely satisfying craft. You will learn techniques for layering, rubber-stamping and embossing, applying eyelets and brads, and embellishing with ribbons and trinkets. While you will need a flat surface to work on, card-making supplies can be contained in a compact carrying box, allowing you to take and make cards on visits or vacations.

4

BASIC SUPPLIES & TOOLS

These certainly do not ALL need to be acquired in order to begin. When you travel, bring along only what you will need for each particular project.

- ⅛" and ¼" circle punches
- 2¾"-3"-wide sturdy brayer
- Adhesives such as clear industrial-strength glue, double-stick tacky tape, glue stick, sticky foam squares, and white craft glue
- Brads, eyelets, eyelet hole punch, eyelet setter, and small hammer
- Buttons, small, flat "found" objects, and trinkets
- Cardstocks in a variety of sizes and colors
- Clippings from catalogs and magazines
- Cutting mat, mat knife, and metal ruler
- Embossing ink pens, embossing inkpads, embossing powders, and heat gun
- Ephemera such as labels, postage stamps, old postcards, and tickets
- Good-quality sharp craft scissors, decorative-edged scissors (such as deckle-, scallop-, and stamp-edged scissors), and pinking shears
- Inkpads in a variety of colors & metallics

- Lace, ribbon, rickrack, and trim in a variety of colors, lengths, and widths
- Nonalcohol baby wipes for cleaning rubber stamps
- Pencil
- Photocopier
- Rubber stamps: alphabet set, backgrounds, images, and numbers set
- Scrapbooking and background papers of all sorts, vintage or new
- Stickers and adhesive photo corners

HEAT-EMBOSSING INSTRUCTIONS

YOU WILL NEED:

- 8½" x 11" piece of scrap paper for excess powder
- Embossing inkpad, embossing powder, and heat gun
- Embossing ink pen (optional)
- Greeting card
- Rubber stamp
- Tweezers (optional)
- Watercolor paintbrush

HOW TO EMBOSS:

1. Rubber-stamp the image with embossing ink onto the card front, or draw the image with an embossing pen.
2. Sprinkle the entire stamped or drawn surface with embossing powder. Carefully tap the excess powder into container or folded scrapbook paper, and pour back into the jar. If you have sprinklings of powder outside of the image, use a soft watercolor paintbrush to carefully wipe them off. Don't be tempted to blow.
3. Aim the heat gun approximately 2" directly above the freshly powdered

image. Sweep it back and forth to heat the powder until it's raised and glossy. *Notes: You may need to hold the paper down with tweezers or other tool if the surface is too hot for your fingers. The image will be dry to the touch almost immediately.*

LOVE SONG VALENTINE CARD

Sweet cherubs and sheet music are the themes of this gate-fold valentine. Pink is added by hand-painting stripes over the sheet music, while black makes a striking accent. Cherub stickers and a button detail add just the right notes to this charming card.

YOU WILL NEED:

- ½"–¾" pink button with two holes
- 4¼" x 4¼" piece of vintage sheet music
- 5" x 10" piece of pale pink cardstock
- 9" length of ⅛"-wide black satin ribbon
- 20" length of ¹⁄₁₆"-wide black sticker strip or paper (an ink line also works)
- Black inkpad
- Brayer
- Cardstock scrap for heart template
- Clear industrial-strength glue and glue stick
- Craft scissors
- Crimson watercolor paint and small watercolor paintbrush
- Cutting mat, mat knife, and metal ruler

- "Happy Valentine's Day" rubber-stamp greeting
- Paper towel
- Pencil
- Photocopier
- Two 4¼" x 4¼" pieces of two-toned pink floral paper
- Two large and two tiny cherub stickers

HOW TO CREATE:

1. Lay the pale pink cardstock horizontally. Fold the left edge in 2½" and the right edge in 2½" to form a 5" x 5" "gate-fold" card.

2. On the vintage sheet music square, draw a line down the center. Starting at the center line, rule ½" vertical stripes with a pencil all the way across. Use these as a guide to apply a very pale wash of crimson watercolor paint to every other stripe. Blot the paint as necessary with a paper towel so that the sheet music doesn't get water-logged. Let dry.

3. Photocopy and trace the Heart Pattern from page 88 onto cardstock scrap. Cut out the template, using the craft scissors. Trace and cut out a heart from

each sheet of pink floral paper. Cut each of the two hearts in half from between the humps down to the point, using the cutting mat, mat knife, and metal ruler.

4. Cut the sheet music in half lengthwise, using the cutting mat, mat knife, and metal ruler. Using the glue stick, adhere one half on the left-hand gate-fold. Roll with the brayer. Adhere the remaining half to the right-hand gate-fold and roll flat. Adhere two of the matching heart halves to the center of the front. Roll with the brayer.

5. Open the card and glue the remaining two heart halves on opposite sides of the card, so the straight edges align with the center flaps of the card. Roll with the brayer.

6. Affix the black sticker strip along each edge of the sheet music so it forms a 4¾" x 4¾" border. Cut the strip at the gatefold. *Note: I trimmed my sticker strips from a larger sticker strip, but they can also be cut from paper and glued on. You could also ink an outline around the sheet music.*

7. Thread the black ribbon through the button so both ends are in front. Tie the ribbon in a bow. Place a dab of clear industrial-strength glue on the right-hand half of the back of the button and adhere it in the very center of the card front so that the left-hand half will be adhered and the right-hand half will simply overlap the right-hand flap.

8. Apply the two large cherub stickers on the upper left and lower right of the card front. Apply the two tiny cherubs inside the card, one on the upper part of the left heart half and one on the lower part of the right heart half.

9. Rubber-stamp your valentine greeting in black ink centered in the middle of the inside square. *Note: For a slightly softer black, stamp your greeting on scrap paper before stamping on the card.*

HOMESPUN VALENTINE CARD

The gingham, rickrack, buttons, and your old snapshot of a loved one's face give this simple valentine the sentimental feeling of Grandma's old sewing basket.

YOU WILL NEED:

- 1" x 4" piece of scrap mat board or thin cardboard
- 5" x 5" piece of pink floral paper
- 5½" x 11" piece of pink cardstock
- 18" length of pink baby rickrack
- 18" length of pink embroidery floss
- Cardstock scrap for heart template
- Clear industrial-strength glue, glue stick, and white craft glue
- Craft scissors and pinking shears
- Cutting mat, mat knife, and metal ruler
- Embroidery needle
- Four white shirt buttons and one ½" pink button
- Gingham paper (checkered or plaid will also do): one 2" x 2" and one 5" x 5"
- Pencil

- Rubber-stamp alphabet set
- Photocopier
- Small square photograph
- White embossing inkpad, embossing powder, and heat gun

HOW TO CREATE:

1. Fold the pink cardstock in half to make a 5" x 5" card.

2. Using the glue stick, adhere the 5" x 5" gingham paper onto the center of the card front.

3. Using a pencil, draw a 1½" x 1½" square in the center of the gingham paper. Cut out the square through the card front only, using the cutting mat, mat knife, and metal ruler.

4. Photocopy and trace the Heart Pattern from page 88 onto the cardstock scrap. Cut out the template, using the craft scissors. Trace the heart onto the floral paper and cut it out. Using the glue stick, adhere the floral heart into the center of the gingham square. *Note: It's okay if there is glue behind the open square hole.* Let dry.

5. Open the card. Cut an "x" shape from

corner to corner in the 1½" hole, using the cutting mat, mat knife, and metal ruler. Fold each triangle back to the inside of the card to form a diamond-shaped frame. Using the glue stick, adhere each triangle.

6. Trim off an even ¼" from the top, bottom, and right-hand edge of the card, using pinking shears. Do not trim the folded edge.

7. Dip a 4"-long piece of cardboard in the white craft glue and lightly make a glue line along the perimeter of the gingham paper. Starting in the lower-left corner, adhere the rickrack. When you come to a corner, fold the rickrack over to form a neat corner; don't cut it. Using clear industrial-strength glue, adhere one white shirt button over each rickrack corner.

8. Place the large pink button on the front of the card where the heart curves meet. Using the embroidery needle, punch button holes through the front of the card. Thread the pink floss through one hole of the button, and from the inside of the card, thread the floss back through the second hole. Tie the two loose ends into a knot, then tie a simple bow.

9. Open the card. Rotate the 2" x 2" gingham paper to make a diamond. Using the glue stick, adhere the diamond in the center of the right-hand side. Glue the small photograph so it's showing through the hole in the card front.

10. Using white embossing powder and a rubber-stamp alphabet set, emboss the word L-O-V-E, placing one letter in each corner of the diamond around the photograph (see Heat-embossing Instructions on page 7).

EASTER EGG PEEP CARD

Like the classic sugar egg, this card is a pastel confection, complete with a cute bunny! Use your imagination in combining various pastel papers and trims to decorate the Easter egg. This card could also be done in a single color theme for a different effect.

YOU WILL NEED:

- 1½" x 1¼" piece of grassy green patterned paper
- 1¾" x 2" piece of sky blue patterned paper
- 7" length of fancy trim for the peep hole (preferably stick-on)
- 7" x 10" piece of lavender cardstock (other pastels will work fine)
- 12" length of ¼"-wide pastel ribbon
- Brayer
- Bunny sticker (small enough to show through the window)
- Cardstock scrap for egg template
- Craft scissors and scallop-edged scissors
- Cutting mat, mat knife, and metal ruler
- Double-stick tacky tape and glue stick
- Embossing inkpad, white embossing powder, and heat gun
- Five or six strips of pastel paper, at least 5¼" long and 1"- 2" wide
- Four or five 5¼" lengths of stick-on rickrack or scallop-edged trim (regular rickrack will also work, but will have a raw edge at each end)
- Pencil (optional)
- Photocopier
- Rubber stamps: alphabet set and small decorative (optional)
- Watermark inkpad

HOW TO CREATE:

1. Fold the lavender cardstock in half to make a 5" x 7" card.

2. Photocopy and trace the Egg Pattern from page 89 onto cardstock scrap. Cut out the template, using the craft scissors. Trace the egg onto the card front, aligning the left edge with the folded edge of the card. Cut out the egg, leaving the 2½" fold intact.

3. Arrange the different pastel paper strips until you find a pleasing combination. *Note: The widths should vary, and stripes should run both vertically and horizontally for more eye appeal.* Working from the bottom up, start gluing down the strips one by one, butting each edge against the next and rolling with the brayer as you go.

4. Turn the card front over and, using craft scissors, carefully trim off the excess paper to the edge of the egg shape.

5. If you like, add some watermark stampings to the strips with a small decorative rubber stamp. *Note: I used four small diamonds, but hearts, squares, or dots would also work.*

6. Using a pencil, trace the oval window from the egg template onto the card. Cut an "x" shape within the oval, using the cutting mat, mat knife, and metal ruler. Use craft scissors to cut out the oval.

7. Affix a strip of stick-on rickrack over each paper seam, arranging the colors so they contrast with the neighboring papers. Trim the ends to the shape of the egg and around the oval window. *Note: If you use regular rickrack, cut thin (⅟₁₆") strips of double-stick tacky tape to attach it on each seam.* Adhere the fancy trim around the oval, starting and ending at the top.

8. Tie the 12" length of ribbon into a bow. Place a small piece of double-stick tacky tape behind the knot and attach it to the top of the oval. Neatly trim the ends at a slant.

9. Glue the 1¾" edge of grassy green patterned paper onto the 1¾" edge of the sky blue patterned paper so the green overlaps the blue by approximately ¼". Use a pencil to trace the oval window onto the green and blue paper; approximately one-third for grass and two-thirds for sky. Cut around the oval with the scallop-edged scissors, approximately ⅛"outside the pencil line.

10. Center the green and blue paper oval behind the oval window so that no lavender paper is showing, and adhere with the glue stick. Center and affix the bunny sticker on the green and blue oval.

11. Lightly sketch a pencil arch above and below the green and blue paper oval. Use this as a guideline to emboss the greeting "some bunny loves you" in white embossing powder above and below the window (see Heat-embossing Instructions on page 7). After the embossing is set, gently erase the pencil lines.

THANK YOU
BOUQUET CARD

This card uses a traditional collage technique of overlapping images. The bouquet here is taken from a sheet of wrapping paper. Photographs of flowers from magazines would also work well, just color-coordinate the paper according to what flowers you plan to use.

YOU WILL NEED:

- 2½" x 5" piece of tan paper
- 8½" x 10" piece of pale pink cardstock
- 10" length of ⅝"-wide cream patterned (*Merci*) ribbon
- Brayer
- Craft scissors and scallop-edged scissors
- Cutting mat, mat knife, and metal ruler
- Double-stick tacky tape and glue stick
- Flower pictures (enough to cover a 4½" circular area, not including leaves and stems)
- Inkpads: Black, rose-colored, and watermark
- Lace sticker strips: one 8½" and two 5½"
- Pencil
- Rubber stamps: alphabet set, floral or ribbon border, large crackle pattern, and large hand (approximately 4½")

HOW TO CREATE:

1. Fold the pale pink cardstock in half to make a 5" x 8½" card.
2. Ink the crackle rubber stamp thoroughly with the watermark inkpad. Place stamp rubber side up on a flat surface and position top half of card front on it. Roll with the brayer. Reposition to have the stamp cover the remaining half of the card and repeat the stamping process.
3. Measure and lightly mark vertical stripes at: ½", 2", 3½", and 5". Using the rose-colored inkpad, rubber-stamp the floral or ribbon border down each mark to form a "wallpaper" pattern. *Note: Stampings can meet, or slightly overlap.*
4. Using the black inkpad, rubber-stamp the hand image on the tan paper. Cut out carefully, including the line between the thumb and palm.

5. Adhere hand approximately ½" from the lower edge of the card. Be sure to leave the thumb unglued as you will be placing stems behind it.

6. Use the cutting mat, mat knife, and metal ruler to cut two ½" vertical slits, centered ¼" above the thumb. Thread the ribbon through. *Note: If your ribbon is wider, make the slits a bit larger.*

7. Use the craft scissors and carefully cut out flowers from the flower pictures. Be sure to include some stems and leaves, too. *Note: You will need those to create a realistic bouquet.* Cut more than you think you will need because the images will overlap.

8. Arrange and glue the stems under the thumb so it looks like they are being held. Glue a few leaves to the stems, being careful not to add too many.

9. Starting approximately ½" from the top, arrange the flowers in a circular shape with the topmost row in the back, middle row on top of that, and lowest row in front. *Note: This will give you the spatial illusion of a 3-D bouquet.* When you are pleased with the arrangement, start gluing them down from top to bottom.

10. From the inside of the card, thread the ribbon evenly through the two slots and make a crisscross on the front of the card. Place the right-hand tail underneath the thumb. Trim each end in a deep "v." Place a small piece of double-stick tacky tape under each tail and press down to secure.

11. Lightly mark a line ⅛" in from the top right-hand edge and the bottom of the card front. Trim along this line with the scallop-edged scissors, forming nice rounded corners.

12. Inside the card, glue one flower tucked behind the ribbon. On the right, affix the lace sticker strips along the straight edges of the top, right-hand side, and bottom. *Note: Cutting the corners diagonally makes it look a little neater, but it isn't critical.* Using the alphabet set rubber stamp and the rose inkpad, stamp the word "*Beaucoup*" centered on the right side. *Note: If you used plain ribbon on the front, stamp both the words "Merci Beaucoup" on the inside.*

ROBIN'S
EGG CARD

Four different squares make a wonderful format for a card. You can tie together four separate elements by using a common color to form a classic windowpane composition. I have used some vintage papers here, but commercial scrapbook papers could be easily substituted.

YOU WILL NEED:

- ¼" circle punch
- 1" x 5½" strips of paper: one piece of sheet music and one scroll-patterned
- 2¼" x 2¼" pieces of decorative paper: One each of map, metallic copper, sheet music, script, and an allover pattern such as arabesque or scroll
- 5" length of robin's egg blue embroidery floss
- 5½" x 11" piece of robin's egg blue cardstock
- 8" length of matching ribbon (my example is edged in copper)
- Brayer
- Cellophane tape, clear industrial-strength glue, and glue stick
- Craft scissors and deckle-edged scissors
- Inkpads: pale blue, tan, and watermark
- Metal ruler
- Pencil
- Rubber stamps: large crackle-patterned and alphabet set (or, small birdie or nest stamp)
- Small copper charm
- Small fine-art portrait in blue tones
- Small jewelry tag
- Two copper metallic photo corners and two small color-coordinated stickers (I used a postage stamp and an egg)

HOW TO CREATE:

1. Fold the robin's egg blue cardstock in half to make a 5½" x 5½" card.

2. Using the deckled-edged scissors, trim off ⅟₁₆" from each edge of the map-paper square and ⅛" off each edge of the scroll-paper square.

3. Ink the large crackle-patterned rubber stamp with the watermark inkpad. Place the stamp, rubber side up, on the

work surface. Carefully place the card front on top of the stamp. Roll the brayer across the card on the stamp, working from the center outward. *Note: You may need to move the card and stamp again for the surface to be completely covered.*

4. Using the tan inkpad, lightly brush the edges of the sheet-music square, the script square, and the jewelry tag to create an antiqued look.

5. Using the glue stick, adhere the scroll-paper square onto the copper square. Using cellophane tape, secure the copper photo corners to the upper left and lower right.

6. From the edge, measure in 2¼" both vertically and horizontally, then very lightly pencil in a "cross" in the center of the card.

7. Using the glue stick, adhere the four squares to the front of the card: map in upper left, sheet music in upper right, script in lower left, and copper/scroll in lower right, leaving a ¼" space between the inside borders. Roll with the brayer.

8. Using clear industrial-strength glue, adhere the copper charm to the center of the map. Affix the two stickers, one in each center of the sheet music and script squares, and glue the portrait in the center of the scroll square.

9. Using the pale blue inkpad, rubber-stamp the words "robin's egg" in lowercase letters on the matte (not glossy) side of the jewelry tag. *Note: You may substitute a small picture of a birdie or nest.*

10. Measure in 2⅜" from each side and ¼" down from the top of the card, marking each spot with a pencil dot. Punch out two holes through the front of the card, using the pencil dots as centers.

11. Loop and secure the blue embroidery floss through the jewelry tag. Thread the floss through the two holes so the tag hangs in front. Tie off the ends inside the card.

12. Push the two ribbon ends through the holes from the front of the card to the inside of the card, cross the ribbons inside, and push them back through to the front. Trim out a "v" from each end with craft scissors.

13. Tear one long edge from each of the sheet-music and scroll strips. Adhere the scroll paper along the inside bottom edge of the card. Adhere the sheet-music strip on top of the scroll so that approximately ¼" of the scroll paper shows above the sheet music. Trim if necessary.

LAVENDER BLUE
MOTHER'S DAY CARD

Layers of lilac and lavender with accents of silver create the delicate vertical format of this feminine card. The wide organza and satin ribbon forms a perfect holder on the inside of the card for a gift certificate or check—a card and a gift all in one. The color theme of this card could be easily adapted to your piece of artwork. Just think how pretty it would also look in sky blue, soft green, rose pink, or buttery yellow.

YOU WILL NEED:

- 2" x 2½" piece of silver metallic paper
- 2" x 2½" piece of thin cardboard
- 2½" x 8½" strip of lavender/blue antique floral paper
- 3" x 8½" strip of tone-on-tone lavender/cream floral paper
- 7½" x 8½" piece of lavender blue cardstock
- 11" length of 1½"-wide lavender organza/satin ribbon
- Brayer
- Cutting mat, mat knife, and metal ruler
- Double-stick tacky tape and glue stick
- Gray or purple postage stamp
- Inkpads: silver and watermark
- Pearl and silver button or snap
- Pencil
- Rubber stamps: ¼" x ¼" tile, postmark circle, and postmark wavy lines
- Small portrait of a lady in blue or lavender (approximately 1½" x 2")
- Two ½" x 8½" strips of gray or lavender small-patterned paper

HOW TO CREATE:

1. Fold the lavender blue cardstock in half to make a 3¾" x 8½" card.

2. Using the tile rubber stamp and watermark inkpad, stamp a row of squares down the front right-hand edge of the card. Open the card and stamp another row of squares, this time as diamonds, down the inside right-hand edge.

3. Tear ½" from the right-hand edge of the tone-on-tone floral lavender/cream paper

23

strip. Repeat the procedure with the lavender/blue antique floral paper. *Note: These tears need not be straight as some "raggedness" adds to its charm.*

4. Aligning the straight left-hand edge with the spine of the card, glue the tone-on-tone lavender/cream floral paper. Repeat with the lavender/blue antique floral paper, lining it up with the spine and gluing it on top of the first paper. Roll both layers with the brayer.

5. Glue one small-patterned paper strip along the spine on the card front. Glue the second strip partially over the diamond stamps along the right-hand edge of the inside of the card. Roll the strips with the brayer.

6. Rubber-stamp the postage touches with the postmark stamps and silver inkpad on the front and inside of the card.

7. Open the card and measure a 1½" slit in the center of the spine. Carefully cut the slit, using the cutting mat, mat knife, and metal ruler.

8. Gently pull the ribbon through the slit. Attach the left-hand edge with a square of double-stick tacky tape approximately 1¼" in from the right-hand edge of the card front. Wrap the right-hand edge around the card to form a band. Place a second piece of tape over the first and attach the right ribbon end. Trim the loose end in a neat "v" shape.

9. Glue the silver metallic paper onto the cardboard. Roll with the brayer. Glue the portrait centered onto the silver rectangle. Tap each side on the silver inkpad to cover up the exposed cardboard sides.

10. Cut the postage stamp in half. Using double-stick tacky tape, attach one half above and one half below the back of the silver framed portrait. Center and attach the framed piece over the ribbon, approximately ½" in from the right-hand edge on the card front.

11. Press down the prongs of the pearl snap or cut off the shank of the pearl button and attach it to the center-right edge of the portrait with a small strip of double-stick tacky tape. Press down firmly.

DAD'S STORY
FATHER'S DAY CARD

Suede and marbleized papers are used here to mimic antique book-binding. Inside this "book" is space to write a small memento about Dad (or Grandpa), along with a matching bookmark gift. This makes a great card to accompany a gift book, and can be easily adapted as a classy birthday card.

YOU WILL NEED:

- ¼" circle punch
- 8" length of ¼"- to ⅜"-wide ribbon in coordinating color
- Brayer
- Cutting mat, mat knife, and metal ruler
- Glue stick
- Marbleized paper: one 1¾" x 7" and one 7¼" x 10¼"
- Parchment cardstock: one 1¾" x 7" and one 7" x 10"
- Photograph of dad, no larger than 4" x 6"
- Rubber-stamp alphabet set
- Sepia inkpad

- Sienna suede paper: three 1¼" x 1¼" and one 2¼" x 7¼"
- Two vintage stick-on labels, two sets of stick-on letters spelling "DAD," and four adhesive photo corners

HOW TO CREATE:

1. Fold the large parchment cardstock in half to make a 5" x 7" card.

2. Fold the large marbleized paper in half. Fold the large sienna suede paper in half lengthwise. Glue the marbleized paper onto the card so that the folds line up along the spine. Repeat this with the suede paper, gluing it on top of the marbleized paper. With the card folded, roll with the brayer. *Note: Some size allowance has been made for the bulk of the fold, so trim off the excess paper and suede to 5" x 7", using the cutting mat, mat knife, and metal ruler.*

3. Cut the three 1¼" x 1¼" pieces of suede paper diagonally to form six triangles. Using four of the triangles, glue one triangle to each outside corner of the card (both front and back), opposite the spine.

4. Center and affix the larger vintage stick-on label approximately 2¼" down

from the top of the card, centered between the right-hand edge of the spine and the right-hand edge of the card. On top of the label, affix the letters to spell out "DAD."

5. Inside the card, use the four photo corners to center and adhere the vintage photograph on the left-hand side. Using the rubber stamp alphabet set and sepia inkpad, rubber-stamp the phrase "Once upon a time…" on the right-hand side, 2" down from the top.

6. For the bookmark, adhere the 1¾" x 7" strip of marbleized paper onto the 1¾" x 7" strip of parchment cardstock. At the lower end of the bookmark, adhere a suede triangle so that the point is at the bottom center. Trim off the excess paper so that the bottom edge forms an even point, using the cutting mat, mat knife, and metal ruler.

7. Punch a ¼" hole in the center of the suede triangle. Fold the ribbon in half and thread the loop through the hole. Push the ends through the loop and pull snugly. Trim the ends at a slant.

8. Affix the remaining vintage label, vertically, approximately ⅞" down from the top of the bookmark. Affix the word "DAD" down the label.

TEACHER THANK YOU CARD

This is a simple card that you and a child can create together. It makes a wonderful "thank you" that any teacher would cherish. If the child has learned printing or cursive writing, they can help with the lettering. If not, they can participate by doing a drawing of their teacher for the "gift tag" that is tucked inside. This is also a great way to use some of those small class photographs. These instructions are for a red card, but as shown here, the colors of the card and ribbon can be altered to complement the child's picture.

YOU WILL NEED:

- ¼" and ½" circle punches
- 1" x 2" piece of black cardstock
- 2⅜" x 4¾" piece of manila or white cardstock
- 6⅛" x 8¼" piece of red cardstock
- 8" length of 1⅛"-wide gingham ribbon
- 12" length of ⅛"-wide black ribbon
- Brayer
- Cellophane tape, double-stick tacky tape, four sticky foam squares, and glue stick
- Colored pencils or crayons
- Cutting mat, mat knife, and metal ruler
- Four photo corners
- Pencil or black marker
- Rubber-stamp numbers set
- School photograph (approximately 2" x 2¾")
- Three 1½" x 4½" strips of lined paper
- Watermark inkpad

HOW TO CREATE:

1. Fold the red cardstock in half to make a 4⅛" x 6⅛" card.

2. Centered on the three 1½" x 4½" strips of lined paper, have the child print or write in cursive: "Thank you," the teacher's name, "From/Love," and the child's name.

3. Carefully tear across the bottom of the "Thank you," across the top of the teacher's name, and across the two sides of the "From/Love" strip.

29

Thank you
Mrs. Bailey
Thank you
Mr. Beales
From Peggy
EMPIRE INTEGRITY

4. Glue the "Thank you" strip ⅛" down from the top of the card front. Glue the teacher's name strip ⅛" up from the bottom of the card. Glue the child's "From/Love" strip centered on the inside right. Roll each strip with the brayer.

5. Open the card and measure a 1¼" slit in the center of the spine. Carefully cut the slit, using the cutting mat, mat knife, and metal ruler.

6. Thread the gingham ribbon through the slit. Attach a piece of double-stick tacky tape on the back of each ribbon end. Center the ribbon ends on the card front and press them down.

7. Secure the four photo corners onto the photograph with small pieces of cellophane tape. Place sticky foam squares behind each photo corner. *Note: Set the squares in a bit so they don't show.* Affix the photograph, centering it over the ribbon ends.

8. On the card front, stamp the numbers 0–9 surrounding the photo, using the watermark inkpad and rubber-stamp numbers set. Inside the card, stamp the numbers 0–10 above the ribbon and the "From/Love" strip. Stamp the numbers in reverse order underneath.

9. For the inside gift tag, cut off two ⅜" corners from the top of the manila or white cardstock. Punch a ¼" hole ⅜" from the center top of the tag.

10. Punch out two ½" circles from black cardstock. Punch a ¼" hole in the center of each ½" circle to make a "donut" shape. Glue a "donut" on each side of the tag, lining up the holes.

11. Fold the black ribbon in half and thread the loop through the hole in the tag. Push the ends through the loop and pull snugly. Knot and trim the ends.

12. Have the child create a colored pencil or crayon drawing of their teacher on the tag.

GRADUATION
CAP CARD

This simple design effectively creates a traditional graduate's cap, complete with tassel. On the inside of the card, I have used computer text to create a more formal look, mimicking a diploma. Nice handwritten calligraphy would also look great. You can create this card in any school color. The inside envelope can be used to tuck in a check, photograph, or personal note.

YOU WILL NEED:

- 1" circle punch
- 6" length of ⅛"-wide purple ribbon
- Brayer
- Computer with printer
- Cutting mat, mat knife, and metal ruler
- Double-stick tacky tape, glue stick, and one sticky foam dot
- Pencil
- Permanent black marker (optional)
- Photocopier

- Purple cardstock: one 1½" x 1½" and one 12" x 12"
- Small gold tassel
- Two 4½" x 4½" pieces of metallic gold paper
- Two 5¼" x 5¼" pieces of purple marbleized or Florentine paper
- Two 8½" x 11" sheets of off-white paper for printing
- Two gold diploma seal stickers

HOW TO CREATE:

1. Fold the large purple cardstock in half, then in half again, creating four equal squares. Open the sheet, turn it over, and fold it in half diagonally once. Turn the sheet over again. Pull the two creased corners toward each other, then pull the other two corners toward the creased corners. Press together to create a 6" x 6" cap card.

2. Open the card with the diagonal crease running through the upper-right and lower-left squares. Center and glue the marbleized paper to the lower-right and upper-left squares. Roll both squares

with the brayer. Center and glue one piece of the metallic gold paper to the lower-right marbleized square. Roll with the brayer.

3. On the computer, create a "diploma" greeting, making sure that the text will fit in a 4⅜" x 4⅜" space. Be sure to leave room in the lower-right corner for the seal and ribbon. Print on the off-white paper. Center and glue greeting onto the metallic gold paper. Roll with the brayer.

4. Fold the ribbon in half, forming a "v" shape. Attach the ribbon "v" behind one of the diploma seals, then affix the seal and ribbon combo onto the lower-right corner of your "diploma" greeting.

5. Photocopy the Square Envelope Pattern from page 91 onto the remaining off-white paper. Cut out the envelope and fold up all four sides. (See Matching Envelopes on page 86).

6. Center and glue the front of the envelope to the upper-left marbleized square. Use the remaining diploma seal to close the envelope flaps.

7. Close the card. On the front of the card, affix the foam dot on the exact center. Wrap the loop end of the tassel around the foam dot. Using the 1" circle punch, punch a circle out of the 1½" purple cardstock. Affix the circle on top of the foam dot, forming the hat's button.

PARTY HAT
BIRTHDAY CARD

This festive paper hat can be used for a birthday card or adapted for an invitation. The tissue-paper frills and ribbons make this card fun, but also make the envelope fat! The color scheme can be easily changed to primaries—red, white, and blue—or hot pink and black, depending on your party theme. Once you learn the frill technique, you can also apply it to other cards or decorations.

YOU WILL NEED:

- ⅛" circle punch
- 8" x 10" piece of classified newsprint
- 8" x 10" piece of yellow cardstock
- Black inkpad
- Brayer
- Cardstock scrap for hat template
- Craft scissors
- Cutting mat, mat knife, and metal ruler
- Double-stick tacky tape and glue stick

- Four 3" x 16" strips of tissue paper in orange, pink, turquoise, and yellow
- "Happy Birthday to You" or similar rubber-stamp greeting
- Highlight markers: orange, pink, turquoise, and yellow
- Pencil
- Photocopier
- Sheet of ¾" white circle stickers
- Three 40" lengths of ⅛"-wide ribbon: pink, turquoise, and yellow

HOW TO CREATE:

1. Photocopy and trace the Hat Pattern from page 90 onto cardstock scrap. Cut out the template, using the cutting mat, mat knife, and metal ruler. Trace and cut out the hat in both the yellow cardstock and the newsprint. *Note: The newsprint can run either on the diagonal or straight across.*

2. Fold both the yellow cardstock and the newsprint down the center to form a triangular-shaped hat.

3. Punch two holes approximately ¼" in from the bottom-front corners of the

yellow cardstock hat. Cut the pink, turquoise, and yellow ribbon in half. Gather together two groups of three ribbons each—one pink, one turquoise, and one yellow. Place a knot in one end of each three-strand group. Thread the unknotted ends through each of the holes to form streamers. Trim ends neatly.

4. Coat the entire outside of the yellow cardstock hat with glue and after aligning the center creases, press the newsprint hat on top of the yellow hat. Roll with the brayer. *Note: The streamers should come out between the two layers.*

5. Inside the card, rubber-stamp the greeting two times on the right-hand side.

6. To make the tissue-paper frill, neatly stack the four colored sheets in this order: turquoise, yellow, orange, and pink on top. Fold in half lengthwise to

$1\frac{1}{2}$" x 16". Make a tick mark with the pencil every $\frac{1}{4}$" on the cut edge. Using the craft scissors, cut in $1\frac{1}{4}$" at each tick mark, leaving approximately $\frac{1}{2}$" in the center uncut; it will form a "comb" (see the Comb Diagram below).

7. Run a line of glue along the center strip of each tissue layer, gluing one on top of the other. Run another glue line on the lower-front edge of the hat. Adhere the frill and trim it even with the edge. Repeat on the back of the hat to form a frilly trim. Make a pouf at the top of the hat by attaching the remaining frill piece with double-stick tacky tape. Trim off any excess.

8. For the dots, color the white circle stickers with the highlight markers, approximately four of each color. Affix them on the hat front and back to form a polka-dot pattern.

COMB DIAGRAM

FOLDED STAR BAR MITZVAH CARD

This card uses simple origami techniques to create a 3-D Star of David as a focal point. The folds of the star are reflected in the corner treatments. There can be a lot of flexibility with the papers chosen, but I think it's nice to include a touch of silver in the card. The instructions below are for a blue card, but you can substitute pink hues if the card is for a girl.

YOU WILL NEED:

- ⅜" x 10" strip of silver paper (same as star)
- 2" x 10" strip of blue patterned paper
- 3" x 3" piece of sparkly silver paper
- 4¼" x 4¼" piece of blue geometric or striped patterned paper
- 5" x 5" piece of complementary paper in a solid or subdued pattern
- 5" x 10" piece of blue cardstock
- 8" length of ½"-wide (or less) sparkly silver ribbon

- Brayer
- Cardstock scrap for star template
- Cellophane tape, double-stick tacky tape, and glue stick
- Craft scissors and pinking shears
- Cutting mat, mat knife, and metal ruler
- Double-sided silver paper: four ½" x 2" strips, one ⅜" x 10" strip and one 4½" x 4½" piece
- Embossing inkpad, silver embossing powder, and heat gun
- Pencil
- Photocopier
- Pink inkpad
- Rubber-stamp alphabet set

HOW TO CREATE:

1. Fold the blue cardstock in half to make a 5" x 5" card.

2. Trim each edge of the 5" x 5" complementary paper with pinking shears. Using the glue stick, adhere the pinked square in the center of the card front. Roll with the brayer.

3. To make the corners for the geometric paper, mark the center of one 2" side of each ½" x 2" silver paper strip. Fold each side at a right angle so when it's turned over, it forms a triangular pocket.

4. Fit one corner onto each corner of the geometric square. Secure corners on the back with cellophane tape. Glue this square on the center of the 5" pinked square. Roll with the brayer.

5. Trim each edge of the 3" x 3" sparkly silver paper with pinking shears. Glue the square to the center of the geometric square. Roll with the brayer.

6. Cross the silver ribbon to form a small loop at the top with tails approximately 3" long. Using cellophane tape, secure it in the center of the card front. Trim the ribbon ends at an angle

7. To make the six-point Star of David, photocopy and trace the Star Pattern from page 91 onto cardstock scrap. Cut out the template, using the cutting mat, mat knife, and metal ruler. Trace the pattern onto the 4½" x 4½" piece of double-sided silver paper. Cut out with the cutting mat, mat knife, and metal ruler. Fold each side in half (see the dotted lines on the Star Pattern). Mark a dot where the three lines cross. Fold each point up to the center of the opposite side. Fold each point again, up to the dot you have marked. Refold each point to the opposite side and, using the second crease, fold the point back onto itself. To secure the three star points, fold the flaps under each other as you

would the top of a cardboard box. Using a piece of double-stick tacky tape on the center back, attach the star on top of the ribbon's crisscross.

8. Trim the ⅜" x 10" silver strip along one 10" edge with pinking shears. Using cellophane tape, secure the strip behind the 2" complementary-paper strip to form a border. Fold the bordered strip in half. On the back of the strip, run a line of glue stick along the left, right, and bottom edges. Open the card. Adhere the strip to the bottom portion of the card, trimming if necessary. *Note: This will create a "pocket" for a monetary gift, photograph, or personal note.*

9. Inside the card, rubber-stamp the words "Mazel Tov" across the "pocket" of the card with the alphabet set and embossing inkpad, spacing each letter approximately 1¼" apart. Sprinkle with embossing powder, tap off excess, and tidy with a small paintbrush if necessary. Blow dry with the heat gun (see Heat-embossing Instructions on page 7).

BUCKAROO
BIRTHDAY CARD

Yee Haw! A classic pony photograph is transformed into this western-style birthday card for a small buckaroo. This is a modern photograph reprinted in sepia for a vintage look. Metal accents of copper eyelets and upholstery tack heads add to the cowboy nostalgia.

YOU WILL NEED:

- 4" x 6" piece of brown suede paper
- 4¼" x 7" piece of parchment-colored dictionary print paper or classified newsprint
- 7" x 10" piece of oatmeal-colored cardstock
- Bandanna-patterned paper: one 5" x 7" and two ⅞" x 11"
- Black inkpad
- Brayer
- Cardstock scrap for rawhide template
- Clear industrial-strength glue, two ½" x 4" strips of double-stick foam tape, and glue stick

- Craft scissors and mini pinking shears
- Four ⅛" copper eyelets, eyelet hole punch, eyelet setter, and small hammer
- Four decorative antique brass upholstery tacks
- Pencil
- Photocopier
- Rubber-stamp alphabet set
- Sepia-toned pony picture, no larger than 4" x 6"
- Wire cutters

HOW TO CREATE:

1. Fold oatmeal-colored cardstock in half to make a 5" x 7" card.

2. Use the mini pinking shears to trim off ⅛" from each edge of the 5" x 7" piece of bandanna-patterned paper. Carefully tear off ½" from each 4¼" edge of the parchment dictionary paper to create a 4¼" x 6" piece.

3. Using the glue stick, adhere the bandanna-patterned paper the center of the card front. Adhere the dictionary paper to the center of the bandanna paper. Roll with the brayer.

41

4. Photocopy and trace the Rawhide Pattern from page 94 onto cardstock scrap. Cut out the template, using the craft scissors. Trace the template onto the back side of the brown suede and cut out.

5. Open the card so it lays flat, front side up. Place the rawhide piece in the center of the dictionary paper. Use the eyelet hole punch to make one hole in each corner of the suede, tapping approximately three times with the hammer. *Note: The hole should go through all layers on the card front but not through the back.* One by one, guide an eyelet through the hole, turn over, and set the eyelet with the eyelet setter and hammer.

6. Use the wire cutters to snip the heads off the upholstery tacks. Make sure they are trimmed off as close as possible. Use clear industrial-strength glue to adhere one tack head to each corner of the dictionary paper.

7. Carefully tear off any excess around the pony picture. *Note: The final size should be approximately 3" x 4½".* On the back of the photograph, affix two foam tape strips, one on each vertical edge of the photograph. Affix in the center of the suede rawhide.

8. Trim each long edge of the two bandanna paper strips with the pinking shears. Fold in half and glue on the inside of the card in horizontal bands so that the backs of the eyelets are covered. Trim any excess paper.

9. Using the alphabet set and black inkpad, rubber-stamp the greeting "Happy Birthday BUCKAROO" centered on the inside right side of the card.

Bon Voyage Card

Little luggage tags and colorful labels tossed with old photos create the vintage feel of a whirlwind "Grand Tour," circa 1920. The French marbleized background paper ties it all together. Once the tiny tags are made, this classy card is assembled very easily and can be created in different color palettes depending on the labels and background paper.

You Will Need:

- 1" x 1" piece of brown paper
- 2⅜" x 4¼" plain manila tag
- 4¼" x 6¼" piece of marbleized paper
- 4½" x 6½" piece of dull metallic gold paper
- 7" x 10" piece of sienna cardstock
- Black inkpad
- Brayer
- Circle punches: ⅛" and ¼"
- Craft scissors
- Cutting mat, mat knife, and metal ruler
- Glue stick
- Six "luggage label" stickers
- Small rubber-stamp alphabet set
- Three black-and-white travel photographs (approximately 1½" x 2¼")

How to Create:

1. Fold the sienna cardstock in half to make a 5" x 7" card.

2. Glue the metallic gold paper centered on the card front. Roll with the brayer. Glue the marbleized paper so it is centered on the gold paper. Roll with the brayer.

3. To make the three mini manila tags, remove the string from the plain manila tag and set aside. Cut out three 1" x ⅜" rectangles from the tag, using the cutting mat, mat knife, and metal ruler. Using the craft scissors, snip off two corners on the short side of each rectangle to form a "tag" shape. Punch three ¼" circles out of the brown paper. Glue one at the snipped end of each small tag. Punch a ⅛" hole in the center of each brown circle. Cut the tag string

into thirds. Using a third of the string on each tag, rethread through the hole.

4. Rubber-stamp, one on each tag in black ink, the syllables "bon," "voy," and "age."

5. Glue the three black-and-white photographs to form a loose triangle on the card front, making sure that a small portion of each photograph bleeds off the edge. Trim the overhanging edges.

6. Glue five luggage labels on the card front so they cascade down from the top to the bottom. Cut the uppermost label in half at an angle along the top of the card, saving the remaining half for the inside of the card.

7. Glue the three small tags between the photographs and labels so they read "bon voyage" down the card front. Let the strings hang loose.

8. Inside the card, glue the last label at an angle on the upper left, letting one corner bleed off the edge. Trim off the corner. Glue the remaining half of the label onto the lower right of the inside, lining up the precut angle with the lower edge of the card.

WEDDING OR BRIDAL SHOWER CARD

The addition of pearls and netting make an elegant and unique card for a very special occasion. The wide ribbon inside the card is a perfect place to tuck in a monetary gift.

YOU WILL NEED:

- ⅝" x 10" strip of antique patterned paper
- 6" x 8" piece of white or cream tulle
- 7½" x 10" cream-colored cardstock
- 11" string of tiny pearls
- 12" length of cream-colored ribbon (approximately 2"-wide)
- Background "script" rubber stamp
- Brayer
- Clear industrial-strength glue, double-stick tacky tape, and glue stick
- Cutting mat, mat knife, and metal ruler
- Inkpads: metallic gold and taupe
- Large and small scallop-edged scissors
- Pale creamy complementary patterned paper strips: two ¾" x 7½" and one 3½" x 7½"
- Pencil

- Small antique sepia-toned bridal or wedding photograph
- Small piece of gold cardstock or mat board that is larger than the photograph
- Two 1¼" x 7½" pale creamy patterned paper strips

HOW TO CREATE:

1. Fold the cream-colored cardstock in half to make a 5" x 7½" card.

2. Ink the large background rubber stamp with taupe ink approximately 1" in on each vertical side. With the stamp facing up, position the card along the long left-hand edge and press down to ink. Repeat along the right-hand edge. *Note: The center of the card front will be blank.*

3. Trim the two 1¼" x 7½" patterned paper strips along one long edge with the large scallop-edged scissors, carefully aligning the scallops from cut to cut. Trim the 3½" x 7½" complementary patterned paper strip along both long edges with the small scallop-edged scissors. Trim the two ¾" x 7½" complementary patterned paper strips along

one long edge with the small scalloped-edged scissors.

4. Using the taupe inkpad, gently brush all the scalloped edges for an antiqued effect.

5. Using the glue stick, adhere the two 1¼" x 7½" patterned paper strips, scalloped edges out and ¼" from each vertical edge of the card front. Roll with the brayer.

6. Glue the 3½" x 7½" complementary patterned paper strip on the card, centered vertically and overlapping the first two strips. Roll with the brayer.

7. Inside the card, glue one of the ¾" x 7½" complementary patterned paper strips to each vertical edge, scalloped edges in. Roll with the brayer.

8. Open the card and measure a 2" slit in the center of the spine. Carefully cut the slit, using the cutting mat, mat knife, and metal ruler.

9. Thread the ribbon, with the ⅝" x 10" antique patterned paper strip on top of it, through the slit. Center the ribbon ends on the card front. *Note: The ends should butt up against each other and may need some trimming to fit.* Attach with small pieces of double-stick tacky tape, one behind each paper end onto the ribbon and one behind each ribbon end onto the card.

10. Place a 1" round blob of clear industrial-strength glue over the place where the ribbons join in the center of the card front. Gather the tulle around in a

circle to create a small "nest" for the photograph and press the tulle into the glue. *Note: You may need to place a heavy book on top of the netting until the glue sets.*

11. Adhere the photograph onto the piece of gold cardstock. Trim the edges, using the cutting mat, mat knife, and metal ruler so approximately ¹⁄₁₆" shows as a "frame" around the photograph. *Note: If you use gold mat board, tap the edges on the gold inkpad to eliminate the white cut edges.*

12. Gently "drag" the string of pearls through the clear industrial-strength glue and drape them in an oval over the netting. Make sure that the two edges of the pearls meet to form a "necklace" effect.

13. Apply two vertical strips of double-stick tacky tape to the back of your gold-edged photo and stick down firmly on top of the pearls and netting. Let card dry thoroughly before placing in an envelope.

PAPER DOLL
BABY GIRL CARD

I have always loved paper dolls, especially their cut-out wardrobes! Patterns are provided here for two baby cards, a dress and a sailor suit, that you can create from a mixture of pink or blue papers. They work equally well as a birth congratulation card, announcement, or a shower invitation.

YOU WILL NEED:

- 3½" x 4¼" piece of light pink vellum
- 4" length of fancy pink floral trim
- 5" x 5" piece of light pink large-patterned paper
- 5" x 12" piece of pale pink cardstock
- 9" length of ½"-wide light pink picot ribbon
- "Congratulations" or other rubber-stamp greeting
- Craft scissors
- Cutting mat, mat knife, and metal ruler
- Double-stick tacky tape and glue stick
- Large and small scallop-edged scissors
- Pencil
- Photocopier
- Rosy pink inkpad
- Two 3/16" white buttons
- Two cardstock scraps for baby girl template
- White jeweler's tag, patterned ribbon, pink embroidery floss, and a large needle (optional)

HOW TO CREATE:

1. Fold the pale pink cardstock in half with the fold at the top to make a 5" x 6" card.

2. Photocopy and trace the Baby Girl Pattern from page 92 onto two cardstock scraps. Cut out the templates, using the cutting mat, mat knife, metal ruler, and craft scissors. Keep one whole and cut the other one out into the various clothing pieces (collar, skirt, and apron).

3. Lay the pattern so that the shoulders align with the top fold of the card. Trace and cut it out with the cutting mat, mat knife, metal ruler, and craft scissors. *Note: The neck will form an*

49

*actual hole through both sides of
the card.*

4. Trim the sleeve edges with the small
   scallop-edged scissors.

5. Trace the skirt and collar templates
   onto the pink patterned paper. Cut out
   with craft scissors. Use the small scallop-edged scissors for the lower edges
   of the collar. Leave the skirt hem
   straight for now.

6. Carefully lining up the edges, glue the
   skirt and collar pieces to the card front.
   *Note: If the two layers are a bit off,
   they can be trimmed after the glue is
   dry.* Trim the skirt hem with the large
   scallop-edged scissors.

7. Lay out the apron pattern on the pink
   vellum. Use the craft scissors or the mat
   knife and metal ruler to cut out the sides
   and top of the apron. Use the large scallop-edged scissors to cut the hem.

8. Run a very thin strip (⅛" or less) of
   double-stick tacky tape across the line
   where the patterned skirt meets the
   plain top of the girl's dress (1⅛" down
   from the top). Center and press down
   the upper edge of the vellum apron
   across the line of tape.

9. Run a second thin strip of double-stick
   tacky tape over the same vellum seam.
   Place a small square of double-stick
   tacky tape on one edge of the picot
   ribbon. Inside of the card, secure the
   ribbon approximately 1" in from the
   card's edge. Wrap the ribbon around
   the front, pressing down on the strip of
   tape, and end up on the opposite side
   inside the card. Secure the end with a

second square of double-stick tacky
tape. Trim the ribbon edge.

10. Lay down a third ⅟₁₆" strip of double-
    stick tacky tape across the center front
    of the ribbon waistband. Gently press
    down the floral trim on the tape.

11. Using small pieces of double-stick
    tacky tape, doubled over, back each of
    the buttons and press down into place
    on the girl's placket.

12. Using the rosy pink inkpad, stamp the
    word "congratulations" centered on the
    inside right side of the card.

13. (Optional) Stamp the words "it's a girl"
    on a jeweler's tag. Exchange the white
    thread for pink embroidery floss and
    "sew" on the tag just below the neck
    hole with a large embroidery needle,
    making sure the ends are in the front so
    you can finish it off with a bow. OR
    Cut a short length of patterned ribbon
    in pink and attach with double-stick
    tacky tape (glue is too lumpy) to form
    a small "label."

PAPER DOLL
BABY BOY CARD

YOU WILL NEED:

- ⅛" circle punch
- 3" x 5" piece of light blue small-patterned paper
- 5" x 5" piece of light blue large-patterned paper
- 5" x 12" piece of white cardstock
- 9" length of ½"-wide light blue striped ribbon
- Craft scissors
- "Congratulations" or other rubber-stamp greeting
- Cutting mat, mat knife, and metal ruler
- Double-stick tacky tape and glue stick
- Light blue inkpad
- Pencil
- Photocopier
- Two ⅜" light blue buttons
- Two cardstock scraps for baby boy template
- White jeweler's tag, patterned ribbon, blue embroidery floss, and a large needle (optional)

HOW TO CREATE:

1. Fold the white cardstock in half with the fold at the top to make a 5" x 6" card.

2. Photocopy and trace the Baby Boy Pattern from page 93 onto two cardstock scraps. Cut out the templates, using the cutting mat, mat knife, metal ruler, and craft scissors. Keep one whole and cut the other one out into the various clothing pieces (shirt, collar, pants, and cuffs).

3. Lay the pattern so that the shoulders align with the top fold of the card. Trace and cut it out with the cutting mat, mat knife, metal ruler, and craft scissors *Note: The neck will form an actual hole through both sides of the card.*

4. Trace the shirt and cuff templates onto the small-patterned paper. Cut out with the mat knife and metal ruler. Trace the collar and pants out on the large-patterned paper. Cut out, using the mat knife and metal ruler for the straight edges and using the craft scissors on the curve of the legs.

5. Carefully lining up the edges, glue all the clothing parts to the card front.

Note: If the two layers are a bit off, they can be trimmed after the glue is dry.

6. Punch two ⅛" holes ¼" below the "v" point of the collar. Thread the blue striped ribbon through, starting in the front to form a "loop-de-loop." Adjust ribbon to make a plump "knot" and trim the ends either diagonally or in a "v" shape.

7. Using small pieces of double-stick tacky tape, doubled over, back each of the buttons and press down into place for the suspenders.

8. Using the light blue inkpad, stamp the word "congratulations" centered on the inside right side of the card.

9. (Optional) Stamp the words "it's a boy" on a jeweler's tag. Exchange the white thread for blue embroidery floss and "sew" on the tag just below the neck hole with a large embroidery needle, making sure the ends are in the front so you can finish it off with a bow. OR Cut a short length of patterned ribbon in blue and attach with double-stick tacky tape (glue is too lumpy) to form a small "label."

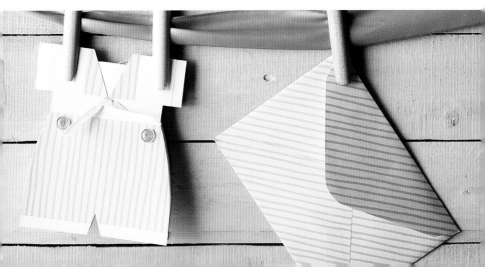

PAIR OF HEARTS
ANNIVERSARY CARD

Cards are a great way to use an old deck of cards! Once you start, you'll find lots of great uses for those Aces and one-eyed Jacks. This anniversary card features the King and Queen of Hearts and makes use of some old cancelled stamps as well. This pair would also be a good theme for an adult valentine.

YOU WILL NEED:

- 4¼" x 6¼" piece of black paper
- 5¼" x 7½" piece of two-toned red diamond or similar geometric-patterned paper
- 7½" x 10½" sheet of red cardstock
- 30" length of ⅛"-wide black grosgrain ribbon
- Black inkpad
- Clear industrial-strength glue, glue stick, and four sticky foam squares
- Cutting mat, mat knife, and metal ruler
- Five or six red-toned postage stamps (either real ones or stickers)
- Gold theme-related charm (approximately 3/4" across)
- Large and small pinking shears
- Pencil
- Rubber stamps: alphabet set and small heart
- Three playing cards: King, Queen, and Two of Hearts
- Two scraps of black-and-red patterned paper (approximately 1½" x 2½" each)

HOW TO CREATE:

1. Fold the red cardstock in half to make a 5¼" x 7½" card.

2. Trim off 1/8" from all four edges of the black paper, using the large pinking shears. Trim off ⅛" from three sides of each piece of black-and-red patterned paper, using the small pinking shears.

3. Using the glue stick, adhere the red diamond paper onto the card front. Adhere the trimmed black paper in the center of the diamond paper.

4. Without gluing, arrange the King and Queen cards at angles and slightly overlapping. *Note: It's fine for a corner or two*

54

of the cards to be over the black edges.

5. Arrange the postage stamps, charm, and black-and-red patterned paper at angles around and under the playing cards. *Note: It often looks nice to group a couple of the stamps together.*

6. Using the glue stick, carefully adhere all the pieces, except the King and the charm.

7. Turn the King card over and attach four foam squares, one in each corner of the card. *Note: Set the squares in a bit to so they don't show.* Press it down on the card so it will "float" a little above the surface.

8. Tap the edges of the card onto the black inkpad. *Note: This will both cover up any white edges and add a more "finished" look to the card.*

9. Open the card. Carefully cut a _" slit in the card's spine 2⅛" from the bottom,

using the cutting mat, mat knife, and metal ruler.

10. Pull the ribbon through the slit, bringing the inside end around to the top right-hand corner of the card front. Bring the outside end down, around to the inside, and around to the top right-hand corner of the card front. Making sure the ribbon is lying flat on the inside the card, tie the ends into a bow. Trim the ends evenly.

11. On the inside left side of the card, adhere the Two of Hearts card at an angle underneath the two diagonal ribbon bands.

12. On the inside right side of the card, rubber-stamp the words "WHAT A PAIR!" and a couple of small hearts.

13. Place a dab of clear industrial-strength glue on the back of the charm and adhere it to the front of the card. Let dry.

COMFY QUILT
GET WELL CARD

This card has a special look because of its dimensionality. The key is to fold each piece of paper just like you would the bedding on a real bed. No brayer is used here; the papers should have a looser look. I have used a bit of crocheted lace and Victorian images for this example, but a primary-colored quilt pattern with crisp white eyelet lace would work just as well.

YOU WILL NEED:

- ⅛"-wide cream satin ribbon pieces: one 3½" and one 6½"
- 3¼" x 4½" piece of a complementary cream patterned paper
- 3½" x 6" piece of muted cream patterned paper
- 6" x 6" piece of quilt-patterned paper in muted tones
- 6¼" length of 1" or wider lace
- 8" x 10" piece of oatmeal-colored cardstock

- Cellophane tape, double-stick tacky tape, and four sticky foam squares
- Craft scissors and scallop-edged scissors
- "Feel better soon" rubber-stamp greeting
- Large embroidery needle
- Manila cardstock pieces: one 2¼" x 3½" and one 5" x 8"
- Paper clippings: face (at least 2¼" long) and a few other images for the bed such as a book, kitty, puppy, teddy bear, and toy (these can be photographs, stickers, or clippings)
- Sepia inkpad

HOW TO CREATE:

1. Fold the oatmeal cardstock in half to make a 5" x 8" card.

2. Position the 3½" x 6" muted cream patterned paper lengthwise on the top of the 5" x 8" piece of manila cardstock, so ½" extends beyond the top, left-, and right-hand sides. Fold the excess ½" edges to the back side, carefully folding the corners in a neat angle. Secure with cellophane tape to create a "sheet."

3. Repeat this process with the quilt-patterned paper, placing it on the bottom of the manila cardstock to create a "quilt."

4. Repeat this process, placing the 3¼" x 4½" complementary cream patterned paper over the 2¼" x 3½" manila cardstock. Leave the left-hand edge open to create a "pillow." Trim the open edge with the scallop-edged scissors to make a pretty pillowcase.

5. Wrap the 3½" satin ribbon around the pillowcase, approximately ½" in from the left-hand edge and secure the ends on the back with cellophane tape.

6. Affix the sticky foam squares to the back corners of the pillow. *Note: Set the squares in a bit to so they don't show.* Center the pillow on the top "sheet" and press down firmly.

7. Using the needle, thread the 6½" satin ribbon through the holes in the lace.

8. Align the upper edge of the lace with the top of the quilt. Wrap the edges of the lace to the back and secure with double-stick tacky tape. *Note: This may be a little bit bulky depending on the lace.*

9. Carefully trim the face and other images. Tuck the images under the quilt, between the pillow and the lace edge. Secure each one with a small piece of cellophane tape at the bottom only. The images should be loose at the top.

10. Flip the entire bed over. Place a small piece of double-stick tacky tape over each lace edge and run strips of double-stick tacky tape around the perimeter of the rest of the bed. Turn back over, line the bed up with the front of the oatmeal card, and press down the edges.

11. On the inside of the card, rubber-stamp the greeting "feel better soon" in sepia ink on the center right. *Note: If you like, add one more "comforting" image to the inside.*

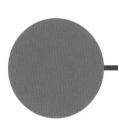

BLACK AND IVORY CARD

Think piano keys, dominoes, playing cards, and old sheet music and you will understand the classic appeal of black and ivory. We incorporate a variety of elements to play out this theme on a big, beautiful card.

YOU WILL NEED:

- 3" x 3" piece of sheet music
- 6" length of narrow ivory/black ribbon
- 6" x 9" piece of black cardstock
- 6" x 9" piece of ivory cardstock
- Black inkpad
- Brayer
- Clear industrial-strength glue and glue stick
- Craft scissors and tiny pinking shears
- Four ½" x 6" strips of black/ivory striped patterned paper
- Rubber stamps: face and shipping label
- Stick-on alphabet letters reading "black" and "ivory"

- Three black-and-white postage stamps (can be photocopies)
- Three small black-and-white vintage photographs
- Trinkets: button, feather, old watch face, tiny domino

HOW TO CREATE:

1. Lay the black cardstock on a flat surface horizontally. Fold the left edge in 3". Lay the ivory cardstock on a flat surface horizontally. Fold the right edge in 3". Using the glue stick, adhere the 6" x 6" section of the ivory cardstock over the 6" x 6" section of the black cardstock, creating a 6" x 6" card with two "doors" on the front, black on left, ivory on right.

2. Using the black inkpad, rubber-stamp the "face" image onto the right-hand edge of the ivory front flap. Stamp the label image so it bleeds off the left-hand edge of the ivory front flap. Inside the card, stamp these same two images on the ivory paper on the inside, with the face image bleeding into the black paper area.

3. Tear the left-hand and lower edges of the sheet-music square. Glue the straight edges to the upper right-hand corner of the ivory front flap. Roll with the brayer.

4. Glue one postage stamp to the center right edge of the ivory front flap.

5. With the tiny pinking shears, trim $\frac{1}{16}$" from one long edge of two $\frac{1}{2}$" x 6" black and ivory patterned paper strips. On the closed card, glue the two strips to the outer left- and right-hand edges, straight edges to the outside. Open the card. Glue the remaining two strips to the outer right- and left-hand edges of the inner flaps.

6. Close the card. Adhere one remaining postage stamp to the bottom of the black flap. Adhere the remaining postage stamp near the top of the black flap, leaving enough space at the top for the alphabet "black" stickers.

7. Carefully tear off the edges of the three photographs. Glue the largest photo-graph on the left and the smaller two on right of the closed card to balance the composition of the three stamps. *Note: The photographs look best when overlapping either the postage stamps or the rubber-stamped image.* Roll with the brayer.

8. Using the clear industrial-strength glue, attach a loop of ribbon in the center of the front black flap so that the loop overlaps the ivory side and the ends flow onto the black side. Trim ends into points.

9. Select your favorite trinket and adhere it with the clear industrial-strength glue over the point where the ribbon crosses itself.

10. Evenly adhere the words "black" on the upper left and "ivory" on the lower right of the closed card.

11. Arrange and adhere the remaining trin-kets. *Note: Don't be afraid to overlap other images.*

LEONARDO'S MUSE CARD

This pretty Florentine card has a design that wraps around from front to back. Mona Lisa looks like she's musing about something—perfect for a "thinking of you" card.

YOU WILL NEED:

- 1⅛" x 2" picture of the Mona Lisa
- 1⅝" x 2¼" piece of thin cardboard
- 2¼" x 7" piece of Italian script paper
- 3" x 7" piece of black/brown Florentine or woodblock paper
- 5¼" x 6½" piece of speckled kraft-colored cardstock
- 7" length of ¼"-wide brown/black grosgrain-type ribbon
- Brayer
- Craft scissors
- Cutting mat, mat knife, and metal ruler
- Double-stick tacky tape, glue stick, and four sticky foam squares
- Four small letter tiles spelling "M-U-S-E"
- Gold "diploma" medallion sticker
- Gold embossing powder (optional)
- Gold metal charm, no larger than ¾" x ¾"
- Metallic gold paper: one 1" x 1¼" and one 2½" x 3"
- Pencil
- Sepia inkpad
- Two 7" black/gold striped sticker strips

HOW TO CREATE:

1. Fold the kraft-colored cardstock in half to make a 3¼" x 5¼" card.

2. Fold the Italian script paper and the Florentine paper in half, with the folds to the left.

3. Using the metal ruler and pencil, mark 2¼" from the top of the kraft-colored cardstock.

4. Apply glue to the entire top-front section. Align the script paper with the fold and the top of the card. *Note: The paper will slightly overlap the right-hand edge of the card.* Adhere firmly and roll with the brayer. Follow the same procedure for the bottom of the card with the Florentine paper. Neatly trim off the excess paper from the

right-hand edge, using the cutting mat, mat knife, and metal ruler.

5. Follow the same procedure to adhere and trim the remaining script and Florentine pieces to the back side of the card.

6. Brush all edges of the card with the sepia inkpad.

7. Line a thin strip of double-stick tacky tape over the line where the two papers meet on the front and back of the card. Secure the ribbon over the tape. Trim off the ribbon ends at the edges of the card.

8. Position and affix the "diploma" sticker approximately ⅜" in from the right edge over the center of the ribbon edge. Trim off medallion to the card's edge. Affix the remainder of the sticker over the ribbon edge on the back of the card.

9. Apply the two black/gold sticker strips across the front and back of the card, ½" from the top and ¼" from the bottom.

10. Center and glue the Mona Lisa picture onto the thin cardboard rectangle.

11. Gently tear the 2½" x 3" gold paper to form a 1⅞" x 2½" second rectangular mat. Glue the gold mat over the ribbon band, just slightly above the card center. Affix the matted Mona Lisa to the center of the gold mat with four sticky foam squares, one in each corner. *Note: Set the squares in a bit to so they don't show.*

12. Gently rip off ⅛" from all four edges of the 1" x 1¼" piece of gold paper. Using

the double-stick tacky tape, attach the M-U-S-E tiles in its center. Adhere the entire "Muse" piece to the lower center of the card, just slightly above the sticker strip.

13. For the finishing touch, place a square of double-stick tacky tape on the back side of the gold charm. Press down onto the center of the upper sticker strip. *Note: To eliminate the "plastic" shine of the tape behind the charm, sprinkle just a little bit of gold embossing powder into the holes of the charm, then tap off the excess back into the powder jar. The shine will be replaced by a nice matte gold.*

M.U.S.E.

HAUNTED
HALLOWEEN CARD

Black crows and a harvest moon on a deep pumpkin color make a mysterious Halloween card. Jewelry tag stickers and loose black string give the card movement and whimsy.

YOU WILL NEED:

- 2⅞" x 8¼" piece of terra-cotta marbled paper
- 8" x 9½" piece of deep pumpkin-colored cardstock
- Black inkpad
- Black paper pieces: one ¾" x 9½" and one 4" x 9½"
- Black/orange harlequin paper: one ½" x 9½" and one 3⅜" x 9⅛"
- Brayer
- Craft scissors and pinking shears
- Full moon sticker and six black crow stickers
- Glue stick
- Jewelry tag alphabet stickers spelling out "Happy Halloween" and "To You" (Other alphabet stickers will also work,

simply punch with ⅟₁₆" circle punch to string)
- Three 12" lengths of black embroidery floss

HOW TO CREATE:

1. Fold the pumpkin-colored cardstock in half lengthwise, with the fold at the top to make a 4" x 9½" card.

2. Trim all four sides of the 4" x 9½" black paper with pinking shears. Trim one long edge of the ¾" black strip with pinking shears.

3. Center and glue the 4" x 9½" black paper onto the card front. Roll with the brayer. Center and glue the 3⅜" x 9½" harlequin paper onto the black paper. Roll with the brayer.

4. Tap all four edges of the terra-cotta paper onto the black inkpad, letting it bleed just a little. Center and glue onto the harlequin paper. Roll with the brayer.

5. Starting with the "Y" at the end of the word "Happy," string the letters one by one onto the embroidery floss, carefully spacing them out. Arrange across the card and gently glue them to the paper.

Pull the string so it's straight and let the ends hang loose. Repeat for the word "Halloween."

6. Place the crow stickers so the string ends can be tucked under the birds' beaks, then press down the sticker to secure. Trim the string ends to your liking.

7. Center and affix the moon sticker at the top of the card so that a little of it folds onto the back side.

8. Inside of the card, glue the ¾" x 9½" black paper strip along the bottom edge. Glue the ½" x 9½" harlequin strip on top of it. Roll with the brayer.

9. Repeat the word-stringing process with "To You," tucking the string ends under the beaks of two crows and trimming the ends.

10. Tap all the cut edges (not the fold) of the card in the black inkpad.

WINTER WONDERLAND CARD

These beautiful winter scenes clipped from museum catalogs can be easily turned into "vintage" photographs and used to create a unique seasonal card in a black, white, and gray palette.

YOU WILL NEED:

- 5" x 6" piece of glossy white computer photo paper
- 8" x 9¼" sheet of flecked light gray cardstock
- 8½" x 11" piece of scrap paper
- Brayer
- Cutting mat, mat knife, and metal ruler
- Deckle-edged scissors
- Embossing inkpad, opaque white embossing powder, and heat gun
- Five laser-cut snowflake stickers and seven or eight white adhesive photo corners
- Glue stick or roll-on adhesive
- Pencil
- Small star-shaped rubber stamp
- Three to five black-and-white winter photographs, no larger than 2" x 2½"
- Watermark inkpad

HOW TO CREATE:

1. Fold the light gray stock in half lengthwise to make a 4" x 9¼" card.

2. Glue each black-and-white photograph onto the glossy white photo paper so that each picture has at least a ⅛" white mat showing around it. *Note: Mixing horizontal and vertical photographs is fine.*

3. With the deckle-edged scissors, crop each photograph so a ¼" margin of white is showing. *Note: This technique replicates the look of vintage black-and-white photographs.*

4. Scatter the photographs down the card front, overlapping each at an angle. Use the angles to cover up the less interesting spaces in the photographs.

5. Add one or two white photo corners to each photograph as an accent on the visible corners. For placement, use a pencil to mark the corners where each photograph falls on the card. Turn over the photographs one by one, apply adhesive, moisten the photo corners,

69

and press down on the paper. Roll with the brayer.

6. Using the watermark inkpad, randomly rubber-stamp stars in the blank spaces around the photographs. *Note: Start sparingly, as you can always add more.*

7. Cut one snowflake sticker in half with the cutting mat, mat knife, and metal ruler. Apply these two halves and three whole stickers to the card front, filling in the blank areas. *Note: It's fine to have them cover over some of the star stampings.* Have each sticker come off an edge, even if it's just a little bit, to create a more natural look. Save the fifth sticker for the inside of the card.

8. With the deckle-edged scissors, trim off ⅛" from the right-hand edge of the card, cutting through both layers at once.

9. For the embossed edges, fold the piece of scrap paper in half lengthwise. Sprinkle a line of white embossing powder along the fold. Tap one deckled edge of the card on the embossing inkpad, then tap in the powder line so the entire edge is covered. Heat-set to create a "snowy" edge (see Heat-embossing Instructions on page 7). Repeat this process with the remaining deckled edge.

10. Using the rubber-stamp alphabet set, repeat the embossing process for your inside seasonal greeting.

11. Add the last snowflake sticker above or below the greeting and accent it with a few more watermark star stampings "falling" down the inside of the card.

DUTCH STILL-LIFE
THANKSGIVING CARD

Large and lush, this card uses a Dutch master painting as its focal point. Doubled ribbons and layers of paper, rubber-stamping, and stickers add to the richness of this card. The colors of the painting are picked up in the background papers, copper trim, and purple-black grapes. You can begin with any Dutch still-life postcard and use it as your color guide.

YOU WILL NEED:

- 4" x 5" piece of metallic copper paper
- 5" x 6" piece of earth-toned floral paper
- 8½" x 11" sheet of sienna brown cardstock
- Brayer
- Craft scissors and deckle-edged scissors
- Cutting mat, mat knife, and metal ruler
- Double-stick tacky tape and glue stick
- Dutch still-life postcard (approximately 3½" x 4¾")

- Four copper adhesive photo corners, large purple-black grape sticker, and several grape leaf stickers
- Inkpads: brown and black
- Pencil
- Rubber stamps: grape cluster, "Happy Thanksgiving" greeting, large crackle background, and watermark insignia (optional)
- Two 1" x 5" strips of dark green/gold metallic patterned paper
- Two 10" lengths of ribbon: one 1"-wide olive green grosgrain and one ½"-wide copper

HOW TO CREATE:

1. Fold the sienna brown cardstock in half to make a 5½" x 8½" card.

2. Trim ½" from the right-hand edge of the card front. Trim a ¹⁄₁₆" edge from the top and bottom of the card with the deckle-edged scissors.

3. Turn the crackle stamp rubber side up and ink with the brown inkpad. Line up the upper half of the card onto the stamp and roll with the brayer. Repeat

on the lower half. *Note: This need not be perfect as the seam will be covered.* Open the card and rubber-stamp just a bit of crackle pattern into each corner, pressing the stamp with your fingers for an "imperfect" look.

4. Using the brown inkpad, gently brush ink on all the card edges, deckled and straight, to create an "antique document" effect.

5. With the grape cluster rubber stamp and black inkpad, add a few stampings to the outer edges of both the front and the inside of the card. *Note: If you bleed the images off the edges, it will give the card a less contrived look.*

6. With deckle-edged scissors, trim a ⅟₁₆" edge from one 5" side of each green/gold paper strip. Glue one of the green/gold strips behind each 5" side of the floral paper so that ½" of the green/gold strip can be seen. Adhere the entire piece centered on the card front.

7. Open the card and measure a 1" slit in the center of the spine. Carefully cut the slit, using the cutting mat, mat knife, and metal ruler.

8. Slip both lengths of ribbon through this slit, the wider green behind and the narrower copper on top. Adjust so that the two ends meet in the center front of the card. Using a square of double-stick tacky tape, pull the green ribbon fairly taut and attach. Repeat with the copper ribbon on top of the green.

9. Trim the postcard so that when placed on the copper metallic paper, approxi-mately ⅛" will show around all four sides to form a pretty copper mat.

10. Glue the entire back of the postcard. Gently place the four copper photo corners on the postcard. Moisten each photo corner and adhere the entire piece onto the copper paper. Roll with the brayer.

11. Glue the copper "framed" art in the center of the floral paper, on top of the two ribbons.

12. Slice the grape cluster and the grape leaf stickers in half vertically, using the cutting mat, mat knife, and metal ruler. Affix one half of a grape sticker and one half of a leaf sticker on the inside left and right edges.

13. For the finishing touch, rubber-stamp in black "Happy Thanksgiving" on the inside right of the card and, if you like, the watercolor insignia on the lower left.

HANUKKAH
LIGHTS CARD

Candles are an enduring image for Hanukkah, and this card conveys that warmth in a simple, graphic style. Shown here in a two-toned blue color palette, this card is also a great way to use up smaller scraps of complementary papers for the candles. This candle design can also be used to great effect for an elegant birthday card.

YOU WILL NEED:

- 1" x 4½" strip of complementary blue patterned paper for inside
- 7¾" x 9" piece of dark or medium blue cardstock
- Brayer
- Craft scissors
- Cutting mat, mat knife, and metal ruler
- Eight 1" x 3½" strips of complementary blue patterned papers (repeats are fine)
- Embossing ink pen, silver embossing powder, and heat gun
- Four 1⅛" x 4" strips of light blue cardstock
- Glue stick
- Pencil
- Rubber-stamp alphabet set, no larger than ½"
- Silver felt-tipped pen
- Small paintbrush (optional)

HOW TO CREATE:

1. Fold the dark or medium blue card-stock in half lengthwise to make a 3⅞" x 9" card.

2. Mark eight 1⅛" sections across the card front.

3. Glue the four lighter blue cardstock strips at alternating 1⅛" intervals, forming a pattern of two-toned blue stripes. Roll the strips with the brayer. Trim off the excess paper along the bottom edge of the card, using the cutting mat, mat knife, and metal ruler.

4. Trim the 3½" patterned papers into eight "candles" of varying sizes. Taper the shapes so that the top is narrower than the bottom. Trim the 4½" strip to form a longer ninth candle for the inside.

5. Glue the eight shorter candles to the card front with the tallest ones in the

center. Align the bottom of each candle with the bottom edge of the card. Roll the candles with the brayer.

6. On the inside, glue the ninth candle slanted from the left-hand side toward the top, bleeding off the edge with the wick toward the center. Roll with the brayer.

7. Use the silver felt-tipped pen to draw small arcs that will form each candle's wick.

8. With the embossing pen, draw an elongated teardrop shape flowing off to the right, above the first silver "wick," to form a windblown flame. Sprinkle with embossing powder, tap off excess and tidy with a small paintbrush if necessary. Blow dry with the heat gun (see Heat-embossing Instructions on page 10). Repeat the process for all candles. *Note: My flame for the inside candle is going straight up, as if being used to light the others.*

9. From the rubber-stamp alphabet set, pull out all the letters needed to spell HANUKKAH. One at a time, emboss each letter on a candle across the card front, tilting each slightly for a more casual effect.

10. Inside the card, draw a pencil line lightly across the center. Use this as a guideline to rubber-stamp the words "HAVE A HAPPY ONE." Emboss the greeting, as above. *Note: Be sure to stamp and emboss not more that one or two letters at a time, so the ink doesn't dry out.* Gently erase the pencil line.

RENAISSANCE ANGEL CHRISTMAS CARD

Once you get the hang of the steps, this small elegant Christmas card can be easily set up in an "assembly line" to make multiples for your Christmas card list. I save the angels and Madonnas from every museum catalog that I receive in the mail and have also found that there are some lovely "fine art" angel stickers on the market. This card can be made in several different color palettes, depending on the central artwork and is a great way to use up small pieces of leftover paper. Experiment and you'll be surprised to find what beautiful combinations you can come up with.

YOU WILL NEED:

- ¾" x 5½" strip of burgundy velveteen paper
- ⅛" x 5½" strip of metallic gold paper
- 2" x 5½" piece of deep red floral paper
- 5" x 5½" piece of metallic gold/red arabesque rice paper

- 5½" x 8½" piece of dark red cardstock
- 8½" x 11" piece of scrap paper
- 12" length of ¾"-wide burgundy satin ribbon
- Brayer
- Clear industrial-strength glue, double-stick tacky tape, four sticky foam squares, and glue stick
- Craft scissors
- Cutting mat, mat knife, and metal ruler
- Embossing inkpad, gold embossing powder, and heat gun
- Gold inkpad
- Pencil
- Piece of gold paper ⅛₆" larger than the angel sticker or picture
- Piece of thin cardboard ⅛₆" larger than the angel sticker or picture
- Renaissance angel sticker or picture
- Rubber stamps: Christmas greeting and large background script
- Small gold charm (feather, flower, or leaf would all work fine)

How to Create:

1. 1. Fold the dark red cardstock in half to make a 4¼" x 5½" card.

2. Turn the large background stamp rubber side up and ink with the gold inkpad. Center the card front on the inked stamp and press down firmly. Roll with the brayer from the center out.

3. Open the card. Using the glue stick, adhere the metallic gold paper strip vertically along the right edge of the card. Glue the velveteen strip on top of the gold paper strip, aligning it along the right edge, and leaving a thin gold band.

4. Fold the red floral and rice papers in half lengthwise.

5. Tear ½" from each 5½" side of the rice paper to create a piece that is 4" x 5½".

6. Using clear industrial-strength glue, adhere the rice paper onto the card so that the folds line up along the spine. Repeat this with the floral paper, gluing it on top of the rice paper. With the card folded, roll with the brayer.

7. Open the card and measure a 1" slit in the center of the spine. Carefully cut the slit, using the cutting mat, mat knife, and metal ruler. *Note: This cut should go through all three papers.*

8. Thread the ribbon through the slit on the spine. Pull the left-hand ribbon across the card front and, using a small piece of double-stick tacky tape, adhere the ribbon end 1" from the right-hand edge of the card front. Place a second piece of double-stick tacky tape on top of the first ribbon end. Pull the ribbon fairly taut, then press down the remaining ribbon on the tape to form a band. Drape the excess ribbon across the card front and trim the edge at a nice angle.

9. Using the glue stick, adhere the gold paper onto the thin cardboard. Apply the angel art onto the gold-covered cardboard. Carefully tap the cardboard edges onto the gold inkpad to cover up the exposed cardboard.

10. Affix the matted angel art approximately ⅛" from the center right-hand side with the four foam squares. *Note: Set the squares in a bit to so they don't show.*

11. Place a small amount of glue on the back of the charm and tuck it under the center left-hand edge of the angel on top of the ribbon. Press down gently.

12. Open the card. Cut a ⅝" strip ⅛" along the right edge above and below the angel art, using the cutting mat, mat knife, and metal ruler so the velveteen will show behind the closed card.

13. Using the embossing inkpad, rubber-stamp your greeting onto the inside right side. Quickly sprinkle the gold embossing powder onto the stamped greeting so it is completely covered. Tap off the excess powder onto a sheet of scrap paper, then pour the powder back in to its jar. Heat-set the greeting (see Heat-embossing Instructions on page 7).

TAGS

The tag examples you see here generally follow the 1-2-3 design principle. Each one features ONE central image, TWO background papers, and THREE embellishments. While all of these tags follow the same basic instructions, you can see the wide variety of looks that can be created simply by assembling different paper and picture combinations. Making a tag is a relatively quick project, so don't be afraid to experiment with different pairings. What works well together may pleasantly surprise you. Plain manila tags are inexpensive; you can use them as a template and cut out your own from different colors of cardstock.

You Will Need:

- ¼" and ⅜" circle punches
- ⅜" x 2⅜" horizontal-patterned paper strips (optional)
- 1¼" x 2⅜" allover-patterned papers
- 2⅜" x 3" vertical-patterned papers
- 2⅜" x 4¼" manila tags
- 5"–14" lengths of cord, ribbon, and string, no more than ⅜" wide
- Brayer
- Buttons, charms, small, flat "found" objects, and trinkets
- Craft scissors
- Clear industrial-strength glue, double-stick tacky tape, and glue stick
- Inkpads in a variety of colors and metallics (optional)
- Metal ruler
- Pencil
- Rubber stamps (optional)
- Small square photographs and a variety of stickers

How to Create:

1. Measure up 3" from the bottom of the tag and mark with a pencil and metal ruler.
2. Using the glue stick, lightly coat one side of the manila tag.
3. Adhere the 2⅜" x 3" paper to the lower

portion of tag. *Note: I love the look of a stripe-oriented paper here, but large-scale allover-patterned papers work well, too.* Adhere the 2⅜" x 1¼" paper to the upper portion of tag. Align the two papers at the 3" dividing line; butt against each other and press down. Roll with the brayer.

4. Glue a ⅜" horizontal paper strip to the bottom edge (optional).

5. If you would like the paper to have an antique look, gently brush from the

edge inward with a vanilla- or taupe-colored inkpad. If you would like to add a darker-colored edge, tap edge of tag onto inkpad so only the very edge gets colored.

6. Place a thin strip of double-stick tacky tape along the paper seam and wrap around the entire tag. Press the ribbon onto the double-stick tacky tape, starting in the center of the front.

7. Add a picture or sticker to front, positioned over the ribbon. If you are using a very delicate sticker, you may wish to apply the ribbon over the sticker so it won't be lumpy.

8. Punch a ¼" hole through the patterned paper on the tag, using the original hole in the tag as your guide. Using a small scrap of coordinating-colored paper, punch a ¼" hole. Turning the ⅜" punch upside down, position it over the center of the ¼" hole and punch out a circle for the tag. Glue the new hole over the ¼" hole already in the tag.

9. Add on any extras—buttons, feathers, charms—with clear industrial-strength glue.

10. Thread ribbon or cord through the hole, first pushing a loop through, then pulling the two ends through the loop. Knot the two ends together approximately 1" from the ribbon end.

11. If desired, stamp a "To:" and "From:" or a message onto the back.

MATCHING ENVELOPES

Many of the projects in this book were designed to fit standard-size envelopes, and there are some very elegant invitation envelopes that you can purchase. However, it's fun and easy to create your own beautiful coordinating envelopes for your handmade cards.

If you find an interesting envelope and would like to replicate it, you can open up the flaps and trace it onto cardstock to make your own template. Avoid using paper that is too thick or you will have trouble getting it to fold neatly and stay folded. Roll-on adhesive makes a seal very similar to a commercial envelope. However, a glue stick or even double-stick tacky tape will also work. It looks great to customize the envelope with a scalloped, pinked, or other decorative edge.

YOU WILL NEED:

- Brayer
- Cardstock scrap for template
- Craft scissors
- Envelope for pattern
- Patterned paper
- Complementary or metallic paper for liner (optional)
- Cutting mat, mat knife, and metal ruler
- Decorative-edged scissors (optional)
- Pencil
- Roll-on adhesive

HOW TO CREATE:

1   Open the flaps of the envelope and trace it onto the scrap cardstock.

2. Cut out the template, using a cutting mat, mat knife, and metal ruler. Trace the envelope template onto the patterned paper and cut out the envelope, using the craft scissors.

3. (Optional) To create a lining, invert the template and simply trace the body and top flap (only) of the envelope onto the lining paper. Trim and adhere the lining onto the inside of the cut-out envelope. Roll with the brayer.

4. Roll adhesive on the inside bottom and side edges. Fold the two sides in first, then fold up the bottom flap. Leave the top flap open.

PATTERNS

HEART PATTERN

100% no enlargement needed

EASTER EGG PATTERN
Enlarge 200%

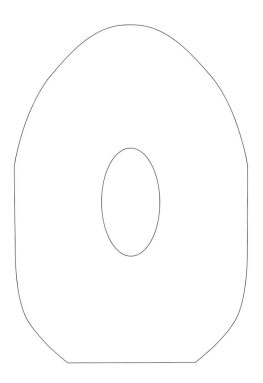

PARTY HAT PATTERN
Enlarge 200%

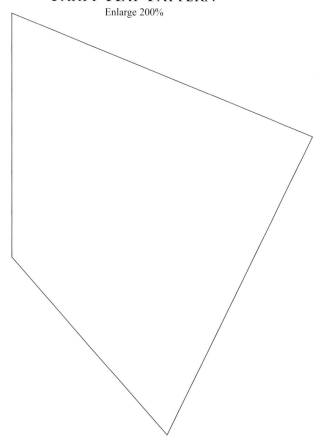

FOLDED STAR PATTERN
Enlarge 200%

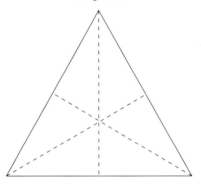

ENVELOPE PATTERN
Enlarge 400%

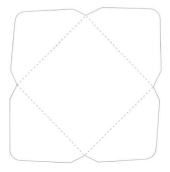

BABY GIRL CARD PATTERN

Enlarge 135%

Baby Boy Card Pattern

Enlarge 135%

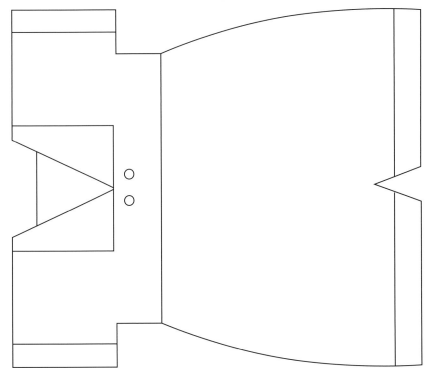

RAWHIDE PATTERN
Enlarge 135%

About the Author

Peggy Jo Ackley

Peggy Jo Ackley began her career as a greeting card designer and later expanded her designs into gifts and house wares. She is probably best known as the illustrator of the *Bitty Bear* book series for the American Girl Company. Since 2002, she has expanded her design work into the art of collage. Always encouraged by her parents, Peggy has been drawing and painting since age 3. She has a degree in fine art from the University of California at Davis and currently makes her home in Marin County, California, with her husband and teenage son.

Dedication

For Donna Garrett and all the happy hours at Attic Archives.

INDEX

METRIC CONVERSIONS

Inches	MM	CM	Inches	CM
$\frac{1}{8}$	3	0.3	9	22.9
$\frac{1}{4}$	6	0.6	10	25.4
$\frac{1}{2}$	13	1.3	12	30.5
$\frac{5}{8}$	16	1.6	13	33.0
$\frac{3}{4}$	19	1.9	14	35.6
$\frac{7}{8}$	22	2.2	15	38.1
1	25	2.5	16	40.6
$1\frac{1}{4}$	32	3.2	17	43.2
$1\frac{1}{2}$	38	3.8	18	45.7
$1\frac{3}{4}$	44	4.4	19	48.3
2	51	5.1	20	50.8
$2\frac{1}{2}$	64	6.4	21	53.3
3	76	7.6	22	55.9
$3\frac{1}{2}$	89	8.9	23	58.4
4	102	10.2	24	61.0
$4\frac{1}{2}$	114	11.4	25	63.5
5	127	12.7	26	66.0
6	152	15.2	27	68.6
7	178	17.8	28	71.1
8	203	20.3	29	73.7